BANGOR

To the memory of my father the late William Wilson who loved Bangor

Friar's Bush Press
24 College Park Avenue
BELFAST BT7 1LR
Published 1992
© Copyright reserved
ISBN 0 946872 54 6

Cover design by Rodney Miller Associates, Belfast
Printed by W. & G. Baird Ltd, Antrim.

Front cover: Children paddling, Bangor Bay *c.*1910
Back cover: Ballyholme, Bangor, Co Down (The Real Photo Series)

BANGOR

Historic photographs of the County Down town

1870 - 1914

IAN WILSON

North Down Heritage Centre

FRIAR'S BUSH PRESS

INTRODUCTION

"Bangor is favourably located at the mouth of Belfast Lough, just where the open waters of the Channel, in all their fresh and wholesome purity, first lave the coast of Down. It lies north-east of Belfast, from which it is reached by road, rail or water. Nature has done much for Bangor but unfortunately, until a few years past, the owners of the estates upon which it stands have not been particularly anxious to devote their time or capital to its further development and artificial ornamentation. This is to be regretted, as, under different circumstances, Bangor would long since have rivalled the most fashionable watering-places which dot and beautify the English coast from Yorkshire to the Isle of Wight. This apathy is, however, fast disappearing . . . " (*The Bangor Season* by W. G. Lyttle, 1885).

Seen today from the sea, Bangor would, at first glance, present to a newcomer a clear image of a Victorian seaside resort. For over two miles, elegant terraces and handsome villas sweep round the twin bays. One hundred years ago most were new, but little appears to have changed since. This book focusses on a period in Bangor's history that determined the character of the town for many decades to come, and has left a splendid architectural legacy. Was the late nineteenth century the zenith of the town's history? Individual opinions on this will differ, but the photographs presented here do much more than show endless picture-postcard scenes of leisure. Daily life and work, and some of the best-known individuals from different social classes, are depicted. However, apathy did seem to be disappearing as the town expanded (and struggled to implement the modern democratic structures needed to cope with its expansion) and the populace shared in the optimistic spirit of the times. Perhaps for Bangor it was indeed *La Belle Epoque*.

Far from being a creation of the railway age and the new desire for leisure, the town of Bangor has an illustrious history. Around A.D. 558 Saint Comgall founded a monastery that, under his austere rule, grew to become respected throughout western Europe. From the abbey — believed to have been on the site of the present abbey church — missionaries carried the Christian message and the civilized skills of reading and writing into continental Europe. The two greatest missionaries were Saints Columbanus and Gall, both still remembered in Christian communities across Europe, the latter also being commemorated by the town of Saint Gallen in Switzerland. Bangor's fame is underlined by its inclusion on the world map *Mappa Mundi* of 1300, one of only four Irish places named. By this time Viking raids had concluded the heyday

of the abbey, although there was something of a renaissance during the twelfth century regime of the great Irish churchman Saint Malachy, friend of Saint Bernard of Clairvaux. Malachy was responsible for introducing to Bangor the Augustinian order, first seen by him in Flanders.

The history of Bangor for many centuries tends to be like occasional sunshine through clouds. Lengthy periods lie ill-documented between sudden revelations of knowledge. Much of the area was laid waste in the second half of the sixteenth century during English attempts to establish colonies, and in 1572 the O'Neills destroyed the abbey buildings to nullify their use as shelter by Sir Thomas Smith's forces. Smith was Principal Secretary of State to Queen Elizabeth I, who granted him a patent to govern much of the east of Ulster, but his incursion proved abortive.

A little over thirty years later, however, came the arrival of the first Scots settlers, industrious followers of Sir James Hamilton, who had been granted lands for services to King James I. Hamilton, a shrewd and ambitious man, advanced his own and his extensive family's interests with a succession of land deals, the imposition of order and the encouragement of progress in what had been a neglected landscape. He can fairly be said to have been the father of modern Bangor. Maps commissioned by Hamilton (first Viscount Clandeboye) show the same basic street plan, the first mansion house on the site of Bangor Castle and many surnames still familiar: Stephenson, Blair, Boyd, Dunlop, Adams and more.

Although Hamilton's direct line of descent soon died out, a descendant, Anne Hamilton, heiress to the Bangor lands, married into the wealthy Ward family of Castleward in 1708. Thus began over 200 years of influence by the Wards over local affairs. Towards the end of the eighteenth century came the energetic reformer Colonel Robert Ward, who promoted the cotton industry as a boost to Bangor's prosperity. Strange as it seems now, two busy cotton mills dominated the seafront giving employment to hundreds.

A pattern in Bangor's history still arguably apparent today is the punctuation of periods of quiet, even stagnation, with short spells of far-reaching development. So in the 1850s and 60s the town's character was greatly altered, first by the closure of the cotton mills, and then, in 1865, by the arrival of the railway from Belfast. Like so many small seaside towns throughout Britain, a new era was ushered in as, for the first time ever, cheap travel was available to the masses. With Belfast expanding at a phenomenal rate, and with the Bangor line being linked to the Irish system, the way was open for the adoption of the role of seaside resort.

Not only did the railway owners convey day-trippers by the thousand, but rooms in new hotels, furnished houses and lodgings were avidly taken by those wishing actually to stay at the seaside, while the wealthier class of Belfast businessman was encouraged to build on the attractive slopes by the Lough side. By 1885, W. G. Lyttle was proclaiming Bangor "The Northern Brighton".

Lyttle, author, journalist and entertainer, makes a splendid guide to the issues, people and general spirit of the times. Until his early death in 1896 he published his own newspaper, the *North Down Herald*. Reference to surviving scrapbooks gives a vivid insight into the pre-occupations of late Victorian Bangor. Lyttle (best known for his 1888 novel *Betsy Gray*) placed no confidence in the town commissioners and tended to lampoon their endeavours, but the issues at stake show that the rapid growth of Bangor and the great seasonal influx of visitors pushed the town's resources to the limit. Democracy had only come to Bangor in 1864 when commissioners were elected to supplant the old Ward-dominated corporation, and the newspaper reveals the job they had to join the march of Victorian civic improvement and provide adequate sanitation, water and lighting. Nor were they helped by anti-social behaviour, a pattern then, as now — or worse:

"On Sunday last Bangor was invaded by drunken toughs. Fighting, in nearly every part of the town, was kept up the entire day, to the annoyance of well-conducted residents and visitors". (*North Down Herald,* 6th June 1890)

The overall picture conveyed as the century closed, however is of a town bursting with fresh ventures, speculations and new-found energy. The population was in the process of doubling between 1891 and 1911, to 7,776 (but swollen ten times at the height of the season). The switchback railway, the Clifton Recreation Grounds, a new steamer pier, demolition and reconstruction on the seafront — these were only some of the talking points as Queen Victoria's reign concluded.

It was in Edwardian times, though, that Bangor flowered fully as a resort. The town commissioners had been replaced by one of the new urban district councils, and financial aplomb allied to a wise assessment of the town's future needs, made this an impressive regime. By 1910 it was claimed that Bangor was the wealthiest urban district in Ireland, and by 1913 it was, uniquely, independent of the Board of Works in the matter of loans, raising money on the open market. Certainly the legacy of innovations can still be enjoyed — the Marine Gardens, Ballyholme Park, Strickland's Glen, and Ward Park all date from Edwardian times. Also benefiting the town in this dazzling era of improvement were the new hospital, library, technical school, grammar school and 'cinematography theatre'!

A new-found confidence seems to exude from the attractive pages of the first official guides which appeared around now. Inevitably, only good things are said (Sanitary Officer Coulter's book of nuisances tells of the darker side), but a glance again at the local press quickly conveys an exuberant mood. Innovations in Bangor and in the world at large abound. The first 'Motoring Notes' start to appear in the press. Aviators demonstrate their flying machines on Ballyholme beach. It is easy to feel that these were Bangor's days of wine and roses. But there was a serious undercurrent to modern life: the Home Rule controversy; increasing European tension; and the excesses of the Suffragettes. The latter's attempts to burn down Bangor railway station in April 1914 would not have surprised the *Co. Down Spectator's* columnist:

"The beautiful, kind-hearted, motherly type of maiden of olden days has disappeared. The tomboyish flapper who brazenly ogles you as you walk round Marine Gardens now reigns supreme..." (22 August 1913)

In *The Go-Between*, set in a golden Edwardian summer, L. P. Hartley observed "The past is a foreign country..." Life after the Great War was never the same. 1914 was the last summer of the old world:

"One local 'nut' mournfully ascribed the rotten weather which characterized this week to 'the big gun firing at Grey Point' ... but what about the Germans? We venture to think that of the two evils our local 'nut' would prefer the rotten weather to the Germans any day" (*Co. Down Spectator,* 16 May 1914)

A few months later, big guns were firing in earnest in France. It was to be more than twenty years until the Tonic Cinema, Caproni's Palais de Danse and the new Pickie Pool heralded a new era of popularity for Bangor.

CHURCH STREET AND BANGOR ABBEY

Bangor Abbey was founded in the sixth century and became a monastic centre of European significance. Although the abbey spire here dominates 'Church Quarter' (Abbey Street, Church Street, and Croft Street), the church had in fact been closed in 1882 in favour of the larger new parish church, before being renovated in 1917. Here the single-storey weavers' cottages are beginning to be replaced by two-storey dwellings, but the barefoot children and primitive drainage present a striking contrast to Bangor's stylish seaside facade usually favoured by photographers. The terraces only continued to the bend at modern Beechwood Avenue where farmland began, through which ran the 'Back Burn' in which Saint Comgall is reputed to have sat for penance!

CATHERINE PLACE AND DUFFERIN AVENUE, *c.*1900

Catherine Place is in the foreground. The name has been incorporated with Dufferin Avenue since about 1900, but is a much older terrace dating from the 1840s–50s. In the mid nineteenth century this was known as the swell street in Bangor. Then it led only to a stream, the 'Back Burn', and fields farmed by Captain McCullough of Rathgael. In a spate of expansion in the 1890s the typical late Victorian terraces of Dufferin Avenue were built in a pleasing arc. The name comes from the Marquis of Dufferin and Ava, North Down's most eminent citizen of the time.

PARISH CHURCH AND WARD SCHOOLS: 'WARDEN'S CORNER', *c*.1910

This junction of Main Street, Hamilton Road and Castle Street could be said to be the heart of Bangor. Nowadays it is perpetually congested with traffic, but here presents a quiet afternoon scene. The present Northern Bank (left) was then a national school — originally being the market house — while the Parish Church of 1882 had only had the spire added in 1899. Older Bangorians still refer to this junction as 'Warden's Corner', from the newsagents (right) run by the eccentric James Warden in later decades. As we see it here, it was owned by his father David. He is advertising his 'Circulating Library' as well as the *Magpie* comic and other publications.

MAIN STREET *c.*1910

This was the first view of the sea glimpsed by the vast numbers who travelled by rail from Belfast. Main Street has always been the chief shopping and commercial artery, but at this time still contained a number of private residences. This photograph can be dated to 1908–10 by the occupancy of the shop (right) which was superseded by the Reading and Recreation Rooms in 1911. At the Imperial Hotel, the famous Mrs Morgan — 'the widow Morgan' — had just taken over as proprietress from Rose O'Leary, a position she held for some 50 years! The building was demolished in 1968 to make way for the Provincial Bank of Ireland.

BALLYMAGEE STREET, *c.*1910

Re-named High Street about 1926, this thoroughfare soon opened out into farmland in Ballymagee townland! The 'Reliance' charabanc from Donaghadee is chugging down the hill, as yet unnoticed by two Edwardian ladies. Note James McKeown's fish shop, still a family-run business today. The low building above Shanks' public house accommodated the gas department of the Urban District Council while the building immediately above it was the Technical School until the new premises in the Carnegie building in Hamilton Road opened in 1910. Ballymagee Street joined the seaside to the countryside in a way scarcely imaginable today.

QUAY STREET, late 1890s

This superb photograph can be dated between the completion of the new Grand and Royal Hotels in 1894–5 and the erection of the present Windsor Bars on the site of the Harbour Bar in 1900. The spacious pleasure grounds in the foreground were a novel feature, unsightly old buildings and yards having recently been swept away. The wrought-iron bandstand was added in 1894 (its cost of £200 being met by the Hon R. E. Ward of Bangor Castle), only to be replaced by the McKee Clock in 1915. It now stands in Marine Gardens, but the delightful Victorian fountain is still there having survived all manner of change around it in a century!

THE SEAFRONT, late 1890s

Quite possibly taken the same day as the previous scene, the process of change from quiet seaside town to bustling resort is crystallized here. Much of Sandy Row (renamed Queen's Parade in 1903) is still dwelling houses, but elsewhere the trippers' needs are in evidence: 'Belfast Prices'; 'Ice Cream'; 'Visitors' Cafe'; 'The Yachtsman'; 'Bangor Cafe'. The role of Bangor as a port is also hinted at by Neill's Pier Office (foreground). James Neill of 6 Sandy Row owned this pier, the coal business and the steamer *Rosabelle*. His successors nowadays trade as Robert Neill and Sons Ltd, Bangor's oldest firm.

BALLYHOLME BAY *c.*1905

The increasing popularity of sea bathing, allied to better rail links with Belfast, stimulated the development of the handsome terraces of Ballyholme from the 1880s on. In 1867 the bay had been described as "the very spot for civilized bathing — but quite neglected". By the late 1890s the long promenade, with steps to the beach below and Ballyholme Esplanade above, had been constructed. This picture would appear to have been taken *circa* 1905, just before the Urban District Council acquired the rough land on the right and laid out Ballyholme Park.

PICKIE ROCK AND BANGOR BAY, mid 1880s

This is one of the oldest scenic views in the book, having to have been taken between the wreck of the barque *Margaret* in 1881 and the construction of the first proper bathing house at Pickie Rock in 1887 by R. E. Ward. However, the first stirrings of the developing resort are before us: Victorian picnickers twenty years before the Marine Gardens were laid out; the rudimentary bathing shelter provided by Henry McFall of the Royal Hotel, and the new sea wall at Sandy Row built by local contractor McFerran. In 1987, ships' timbers probably from the *Margaret* were dredged up during construction of the new marina.

BOATING IN BANGOR BAY, 1904 or 1905

Twenty years on from the previous picture, the bay presents a more animated scene as the aquatic entertainment at Lenaghen's jetty draws the strollers. The old *Margaret* has sunk into the sand, the New Pier (1895) has been built and Bangor is thriving. Note the beautiful little steam launch in the foreground and the children dangling their feet in the water!

An interesting point is that the Belfast paddle steamer at the New Pier is not the regular *Slieve Bearnagh* so often depicted but the elderly *Marquis of Bute* from the Clyde, which challenged the Belfast and Co. Down Railway Co.'s sea service monopoly in 1904 and 1905.

11

STRICKLAND'S GLEN, July 1914

The Glen was purchased in 1913 by the Urban District Council from Colonel R. G. Sharman-Crawford of Crawfordsburn and laid out in the way we know today for the following summer season. The paths and little bridges were the work of men supervised by William Legge, caretaker of Ward Park and resident superintendent of the Masonic Hall, Hamilton Road. Rather earlier, the odd building known as 'The Bungalow' had been constructed to provide refreshments. It was supposedly inspired by Malayan styles! In the background can be seen the Homes of Rest.

THE HOMES OF REST, DOWNSHIRE ROAD

Annually, for an estimated 7,000 needy Belfast people, a week at this healthy spot was their only holiday from the city. A philanthropist named Vance chose the sites of these spacious homes and another at the foot of Brompton Road. The local paper, the *North Down Herald*, commented on 31 July 1914: "to be able to give a man food and lodgings for 8s.6d. a week or a woman for 6s.0d. is the essence of good management . . . and of practical philanthropy". The League of Kindness and Fresh Air Fund helped "White-faced little mortals fading in sultry back streets". Slightly altered, the old homes still fulfil charitable and church-related functions.

BANGOR HOMING PIGEON CLUB,
8th March 1904

The bowler-hatted gentleman in the back row is committee member Fred Clawson, who had an upholstery business near today's Post Office. Sam Johnston (extreme left, seated) favours a Panama hat. He farmed land in Ballymagee townland that was developed in the late 1930s and 1940s and named Beverley Hills by his wife Amy, a keen movie fan! Flat caps are the norm for the other pigeon fanciers who include barber William McGrath of Ballymagee Street (second left, third row). Extreme left and right are brothers John and Harry O'Hara, two of the five sons of Mrs O'Hara of the Grand Hotel. Both later emigrated to America.

Bangor Rugby Football Club, First XV.

WINNERS OF ULSTER JUNIOR LEAGUE, AND RUNNERS-UP ULSTER JUNIOR CUP, 1910–11.

BANGOR RUGBY TEAM, 1911

This was a particularly successful era in the history of Bangor Rugby Football Club, who played at grounds off Brunswick Road — hence the name Rugby Avenue. Third from left in the back row is another O'Hara brother Joe, who sadly died of leukaemia only a year or so later. Centre of the back row is club treasurer F. J. Brice who followed his father James in the auctioneering business. Sitting on the extreme right is Sam Neill a son of James the coal merchant, and grandfather of sisters Maxine (Director, Robert Neill & Sons Ltd.) and Rose (B.B.C.).

THE SWITCHBACK RAILWAY, KINGSLAND

This rare and fascinating picture highlights a great, but forgotten attraction. In season, during its brief life, thousands every day thrilled to the longest switchback ride in the U.K. A Thompson's Gravity Patent Switchback, it was opened in June 1889 by Lady Clanmorris of Bangor Castle, and was the concept of John Moore (operator of the 'Bangor boat') who leased the land from Lady Clanmorris' father R. E. Ward.

Opening the railway, Ward theorized "... going downhill has a marvellous effect, completely taking away your breath, but as you ascend your breath returns with renewed vigour. This produces the most lovely blushes on the ladies' faces and makes them so attractive no gentleman could help proposing" (*North Down Herald,* June 1889). Sadly, the switchback was destroyed in the great gale of December 21–22, 1894.

CLIFTON RECREATION GROUNDS

"The Bangor Recreation Grounds at Clifton present a remarkable contrast to the Bangor of long ago. Thousands of persons throng the grounds by day and night and enjoy themselves with all the ardour of early schooldays. Waxwork exhibitions, switchbacks, swingboats and merry-go-rounds are reaping a golden harvest and the merry music resounds even as the small hours are ushered in. Every age and style is represented from Noah's Ark to the modern cad. One well-known and conspicuous figure is visible at the swing boats. It is that of a burly and genial Belfast solicitor who, with his amiable home partner, goes whizzing through the air" (*North Down Herald,* 5 August 1892).

WARD PARK, *c.*1910

The golf clubhouse can be seen in the background and near it the smoking chimney of the steam laundry (proprietor James McMurray). This charming postcard photograph captioned 'Public Park' shows the new park shortly after it had been laid out about 1909. The actual name Ward Park was bestowed in 1912. The land had formerly been a brickworks and the two ponds are reputedly sites of clay pits. The pronounced slope on the golf course (right) reveals why the houses in present day Moira Drive have back gardens on a lower level, and rear basements.

TENNIS AND BOWLS IN WARD PARK

"Bangor bowlers are real sport . . . and the conviviality and youthful exhilaration combined with the rejuvenescence of those who have passed the meridian of life show how heartily they engage in this innocent and health-giving sport . . . Bangor green is so beautiful with its emerald hue that men accustomed to it cannot endure those greens where barren patches stand in conspicuous contrast to shades that cheer the eye". (*Co Down Spectator*, 24 July 1914). The bowling green was laid out for the 1911 season, with tennis courts nearby, "to cater for the tastes of the better class of inhabitants".

NEGRO BAND, 1893
Little is known of this attraction, as 1893 pre-dates surviving local newspapers, but a caption on the back of the original print states "Coloured Negro Troupe at Bangor 1893, leader Billy Taylor".

CONCERT PARTY AT THE BANDSTAND

"... the inimitable Alex Stewart has made several 'hits' with his rag-time songs. The visit of Mr Sam Hilton and his Donaghadee company on Saturday night was hailed with delight by the younger 'Esplanadites', and once again 'Oh, Oh Susannah' was merrily chanted". (*Co. Down Spectator,* August 1913). A troupe of artists, the Royal Nomads, was annually brought by a Mr Medley Barrett although once season was curtailed following a crowd disturbance when a popular singer failed to appear! Promenading in the foreground are local builder James H. Savage and his wife.

ROWING BOATS FOR HIRE, 1890

One of the perennial attractions of Bangor was the chance to hire a boat and enjoy a row in the bay. The prospect of meeting amateur sailors was less attractive for skippers of the incoming Belfast paddle steamer! Here the slip at the harbour-master's office is in action in the days before the North Pier and before

Dr Moore had built his fine red-brick villa (now the Sands Hotel) on the site of Sally Beattie's cottage. Harbour-master at this time was burly Cornish 'sea-dog' Captain John Tregaskis who was part of the sea front scene for thirty years with his phrase "I knows my dooty" and stick to belabour erring boys!

GOLF CLUBHOUSE, OFF HAMILTON ROAD

This commodious and handsome red-brick building was constructed in 1904 for the new Bangor Golf Club, the architect being Ernest L. Woods who later designed the nearby library. The first fairway stretched down present Moira Drive and a sliced shot would end up in the park! Ladies had a smaller and more humble clubhouse. The present course, incorporating some of the original holes, dates from 1934 when this building became Aubrey House private school. During the war it housed the local A.T.S. unit, then Connor House preparatory school. Slowly disintegrating—occasionally aided by small boys—it was finally levelled in 1970.

BATHING IN BALLYHOLME BAY

This is one scene little changed today and the summer days are often just as chilly! These Edwardians, however, are well wrapped up, and only a few hardy souls have ventured in. The shrieks of the young girls paddling can be imagined! In 1906, the Urban District Council were vexed by mixed bathing at Ballyholme Bay, a controversy to add to another then raging over the rights and wrongs of hiring rowing boats on Sundays.

PARTY AT LENAGHEN'S JETTY

James Lenaghen (centre) was a rowing boat owner and builder who claimed to have the biggest fleet in Ireland. He resided at 'Brookfield', 36 Southwell Road, and his jetty nearby in Bangor Bay pre-dated the famous 'Laird's Boats'. This may perhaps be an Edwardian Sunday school outing. The gentleman in the straw boater (left) was one of the town's best-known characters, Sam Coulter.

THE HARBOUR, late 1880s

This fascinating photograph reveals another side of Bangor life – the small port with its attendant bustle and clutter. For a century after this the working harbour co-existed uneasily with Bangor the resort, leisure use finally triumphing in the 1990s! Note the yards and buildings demolished in 1891, the south pier as formed in 1757 and the hulks used as breakwaters. The limestone on the quayside would have come from Whitehead or Glenarm in a tiny sailing coaster, while the collier dominating the scene is very possibly Charles Neill's *James Stonard*, captained by James Eddis, which was disastrously wrecked in 1890.

QUAY STREET, late 1880s

This photograph can only have been taken within a few years after 1887, when the present Steamer Bar (until 1992 the Marine Bar) changed its name briefly from the Abercorn to the Mermaid. The uses of the buildings satisfied the needs of a small but busy port. As well as the hostelries — the first of three Royal Hotels is centre — Charles Neill's business headquarters and family home is visible at 2 Quay Place (present-day Crosby Street) while the terrace housed sea captains. The original port custom house of *circa* 1637 and protective tower (left) was a private residence. The last family to dwell there were the Keenans from about 1906–1924.

THE BANGOR CASTLE AND OTHER SHIPPING
*c.*1890

The fast paddle steamer *Bangor Castle* was originally built for blockade-running into Confederate ports in the American Civil War. Moore Bros operated her and her consort *Erin* with great success until the Belfast and Co. Down Railway Co.'s new steamers challenged them. Berths at the quay were congested in summer, and passengers objected to the mess of coal, horses etc., so after much discussion over design, the new North Pier was completed in 1895 (demolished 1981). Note the very rare view here of the first Grand Hotel and the old mill of 1806, both on the sea side of Bridge Street.

TWO 'BANGOR BOATS' LAID UP IN THE LONG HOLE

Only the evidence of this extraordinary photograph could convince anyone that two large paddle steamers were squeezed in here for the winter! The *Erin* (left) and *Bangor Castle* ran from 1864 and 1873 respectively, until 1894, making up to eight round trips per day from Belfast '... the Bangor steamers have taken their place as an institution, and any interruption in their season would be regarded by Belfast people as the forerunner of chaos and the approach of those latter days when the sun would refuse his light and the waters leave their beds'. (*The Bangor Season*, 1885)

KETCH NEWLAND: CAPTAIN MONTGOMERY

Captain James Montgomery owned this little ketch from 1877 until his death in July 1896. Similar old craft, Victorian equivalents of big lorries, are berthed nearby. Their crew laboriously unloaded limestone, then by hand took on forty tons of bricks for Ballyhalbert! Another of Captain Montgomery's vessels the *Susan* was wrecked at Troon in 1884 under the command of James Eddis, later to be drowned in the *James Stonard*—such were the dangers of the coasting trade. Larger colliers (left) brought coal from Cumberland, Ayrshire or the Mersey but steam replaced the last one in 1904.

CAPTAIN WILLIAM COEY AT THE LONG HOLE

Captain William Coey (right) was born in 1847, probably the son of another sea captain, William Coey (1816–64). He gained his master's certificate in 1874 and later owned the brigantine *Opah* operating in the coasting trade. By 1892, which is roughly the date of this photograph, he is listed as commanding the deep-sea ship *Elba*. He lived in Fisher Hill, later re-named Victoria Road. Other Bangorians skippering ships world-wide at this time included William Austin, Robert Brown, Mark Campbell, Gilbert Oliver, John Nicholson and two men named Robert Crosbie.

YACHTING OFF BANGOR

For the cream of local society, the Ulster Yacht Club was revived in 1866 by Lord Dufferin and under his commodoreship received a Royal Charter in 1870. Its regattas attracted all the leading yachts in British waters. Two less grand clubs were formed by enthusiastic locals — Bangor Corinthian Sailing Club (1880) and Ballyholme Sailing Club (1900) which was later re-constituted as Ballyholme Yacht Club. The large yachts here, 37 feet overall, are probably of the Class One Belfast type built in the 1890s by Hilditch of Carrickfergus. The sheltered creek in the foreground is beside Seacliff Road.

NAVAL VISIT, 1896

One of the highlights of a Bangor summer was a squadron of warships anchoring in the lough. The Belfast paddle steamers did a roaring trade, the thousands of bluejackets on shore leave set female hearts fluttering, while 'whalers' like these engaged in vigorous rowing races. Such boats sometimes landed men in Ballyholme Bay to obtain dry sand, which was needed daily to scrub clean the warships' wooden decks. The ladies of the neighbouring villas would make picnic teas for the men as the boats lay stranded at low tide.

BATTLESHIPS IN BANGOR BAY

This marvellous photograph evokes a lost age. It was probably taken in August 1907 during the visit of the Second Division, Atlantic Fleet. The battleships are members of the *King Edward* class built in 1905–06. The Marine Gardens, through which people are so contentedly strolling, had only recently been acquired by the Council, while Pickie Pool was then male-only. It is about noon on a sunny day with a light westerly breeze flapping the white ensigns.

On headstone:

ERECTED
BY
THE INHABITANTS OF BANGOR
IN MEMORY OF
PETTY OFFICER THOMAS HINES,
WHO DIED AT HIS DUTY,
ON BOARD H.M.S. "CORNWALLIS"
ON FRIDAY 16TH AUGUST 1907,
DURING THE MEMORABLE VISIT OF
ATLANTIC FLEET TO BANGOR.
BORN 1867. DIED 1907.

GRAVE OF STOKER HINES OF ATLANTIC FLEET

Exeter man Thomas Hines of *H.M.S. Cornwallis* died of a sudden haemorrhage. An enormously impressive naval funeral on Sunday, 18 August 1907, led by the massed bands of the fleet, made its way to the Newtownards Road cemetery. Thomas Matthews, J.P., a prominent local coal merchant and public figure, organised a subscription for this headstone and for Hines's widow. Strangely, the first-ever burial here in 1899 was of a seaman from *H.M.S. Niobe*, accidentally killed on a naval visit. The farm in the background is roughly on the site of Clandeboye Road Presbyterian Church.

GROOMSPORT LIFEBOAT TO THE RESCUE, 1897

On June 16, 1897 during a strong northerly gale, two sailing ships were dragging their anchors off Bangor. The Groomsport lifeboat *George Pooley* was transported on her carriage and launched from the South Pier ('Neill's Pier') by means of skids.

The men then had a hard pull to get to windward of the vessels, the *Harp* of Arklow and the *Hollyhow* of Galway. Thus positioned the boat could be borne down on each distressed vessel by the wind.

LANDING THOSE IN PERIL

The lifeboat first took off four men from the *Harp* before veering down on the *Hollyhow* and taking off eight people — the master, his wife and three children and three crew. This schooner was within 100 yards of Seacliff Road. Course was then set for Ballyholme Sailing Club jetty and the survivors landed, watched by an excited crowd. (In the same gale the first steamer in Belfast's Kelly fleet, *Susannah Kelly* was lost with all hands in the North Channel.)

RAILWAY STATION

Beneath today's bland rendering lies the ornate red and yellow brick of what was, in its day, an imposing terminus, opened in 1865 for the Belfast, Holywood and Bangor Co. Eight trains each way began to run daily and this great innovation became the major factor in Bangor's growth. The company, and later the B.C.D.R. which absorbed them in 1884 offered free travel incentives to those building properties, sponsored firework displays and generally furthered their interests by helping make Bangor 'the Kingstown of Belfast'.

DONAGHADEE COACH NEAR THE STATION,
*c.*1910

James Fletcher's passenger coach is seen outside the site of present day Stewart Miller's shop. Belfast passengers could of course travel by rail to Donaghadee by the circuitous route via Comber, and around 1900 the B.C.D.R. drew up plans for extending the Bangor line through Ballyholme to Donaghadee, but these were never implemented. Fletcher, an undertaker and coachbuilder, established his business at 32–34 Ballymagee Street in 1869. In 1915 he was still advertising for hire "Fashionable wedding carriages, buses, Landaus, Victorias, Cabs and Cars, Pic-Nic Waggonettes, Char-a-bancs etc".

PENNY-FARTHING BICYCLE, 1870s

This fascinating photograph is one of the oldest featured in the book, apparently taken before the new Sandy Row sea wall was built in the late 1870s. A rather military looking gentleman is using a bollard as a step up to his penny-farthing. Again in evidence is one of the tiny smacks engaged in the limestone trade. This could possibly be the *Petrel* owned by the original Robert Neill (1800–73) and his sons Charles and James. On 3 June 1875, when carrying 30 tons over from Whitehead, she suddenly sank, though the crew escaped.

PONY POWER

Mr & Mrs J. H. Savage of 'Mount Herald', 1 Ballyholme Road, were among Bangor's best-known citizens. The extensive out-buildings to the house (the whole site now a car park) would have included space for their little cart and its faithful pony.

Mrs Savage is to the right with one of her sons, Alex, and a Miss Hutchinson. Could she have been the family governess? This variety of cart was sometimes called a Governess Cart.

MOTORING PARTY, *c.*1910

The vehicle is an Argyll, a pioneer motor car built at a works in Alexandria, near Glasgow.—J. B. Ferguson was the Ulster agent. The lady taking the wheel from the chauffeur is probably Mrs Lepper of 'Laurel Lodge', Maxwell Road, a villa that later became 'Garth House' private school. A registration list of 1915 gives her as the owner of 1J 25, an early Co. Down number. She was the widow of Mr F. R. Lepper, a prominent Belfast businessman.

HAMILTON ROAD — THE OLD AND THE NEW

Judging by the unmetalled state of the roads then, it is no surprise that dust was such a public annoyance! (Bangor, though, was said to be an example of well-kept roads). The self-conscious pride of the occupants of the vehicle contrasts with the relaxed demeanour of the boys in the cart. The Belfast registration numbers show that private car ownership was increasing steeply. In 1915 the registered owner of this car was James Campbell, Malone Avenue, Belfast. By this time Bangor was able to justify two motor engineers — Bob McCreadie Limited and Andrew Fulton, both of Main Street. You could also buy 'Motor Suits and Great Coats' at S. G. Montgomery & Co., tailors.

FLYING MACHINE ON BALLYHOLME BEACH, 1914

This wonderful photograph almost certainly depicts the flying display in June 1914 by the French aviator Henri Salmet: ". . . starting in the Groomsport direction the machine rose like a bird on the wing and circled Ballyholme Bay, its progress being watched with the closest attention by the spectators who expressed in an unmistakable manner their admiration of

M. Salmet's skill and daring" (*County Down Spectator*). These thrills were followed by an official dinner for Salmet and his entourage in the Grand Hotel, while thousands attended a military band promenade and fireworks in the Ward Park. Six weeks later, the world was at war.

THE 'RELIANCE' CHARABANC, *c.*1912

The lack of a railway beyond Bangor, and the scenic nature of
the coastline, meant that private motor charabanc owners
flourished in the years immediately before the Great War. After
the war, competition all over Co. Down to the B.C.D.R. eroded
the company's prosperity. Each vehicle gloried in a name —
'Invincible', 'Enterprise' and here 'Reliance', a roofed open-
sided Dennis, which offered trips to Donaghadee and back for
one shilling. The gradient in Ballymagee Street obliged her to
depart via Seacliff Road!

BANGOR CASTLE, *c.*1895

Situated on an airy vantage point overlooking the town, Bangor Castle is at least the third mansion house on this site. It was built in 1852 for the Hon R. E. Ward, the sandstone being specially imported from Ayrshire. The style is the then-fashionable Elizabethan revival. Ward's only child Maude married Lord Clanmorris from Co. Mayo and the family lived here, the children in time numbering ten. The lady seen here could be Lady Clanmorris, or perhaps a governess, with the two girls whose ages were close, Ierne (1882–1917) and Ina (1884–1957).

DRAWING ROOM, BANGOR CASTLE

This room offered pleasant views over the formal gardens, the town of Bangor and Belfast Lough beyond, with Scotland visible on a clear day. The moulded plaster ceiling is very striking and the design continued into the adjoining library.

On the death of Lady Clanmorris in 1941 the family sold the castle and demesne to Bangor Borough Council and this room is now the office of the town clerk of North Down Borough Council as it was re-constituted in 1973.

SOUTH-WEST CORNER, BANGOR CASTLE, 1895
Architectural historians have never been totally certain that
William Burn designed all of Bangor Castle. It seems from the
available evidence that the extensive out-buildings at the rear,
grouped round a courtyard, are the work of Anthony Salvin.
The more medieval style of these buildings, which included
carriage and stable accommodation and a laundry, contrast
with the main house. They now house North Down Heritage
Centre. Here a dapper Victorian gentleman, perhaps a house
guest of Lord and Lady Clanmorris, enjoys a stroll.

HARBOUR MASTER'S OFFICE AND THE TOWER

Two of Bangor's best-known landmarks, both thankfully still surviving, are visible here. The harbour-master's office dates from about 1840 and probably originally housed coastguards. Its basement was formerly a boat-house with slipway but sadly is now severed from the sea. The tower, and adjoining tower house, was built around 1637 as a fine customs building shortly after the advent of the Scots planter regime under Sir James Hamilton. 'Tower Buildings' (left) is a terrace built about 1890 by Charles Neill of the coal and shipping family. It has unusual oriel windows on timber supports at first floor level.

BANGOR ABBEY AND NEWTOWNARDS ROAD

No doubt taken in the period of its closure, (1882–1917), this photograph emphasises how the abbey has remained unchanged while dramatic developments have taken place all around. The proximity of the countryside is evident; the Newtownards Road rises at once into the fields. The main body of the abbey dates from re-buildings of the 1830s and 40s, but the tower is fifteenth century and the steeple dates from 1693. There has been Christian worship on this site for over 1,400 years.

THE RECTORY AND BANGOR ABBEY, 1880

The original photograph is dated 'about 1880' on the back. This huge and rather forbidding-looking house with extensive out-buildings appears on the first ordnance survey map of 1834 as a 'Glebe House' or Rectory. It was demolished in 1932.

There were also a few acres of glebe land to be farmed, both adjacent to here and off Brunswick Road — then known as 'Ash Loanen'. Dean Edward Maguire, a fearless climber, was known to clear nests from his chimneys, fifty feet up.

UPPER MAIN STREET (i)

Surely this photograph must rank as the most difficult to place today! It is in fact the old terrace beside the present Post Office. Bangor Castle demesne extended into the town in a way difficult to imagine today. However, the world of the 'big house' was largely private, although in the 1880s the gardens were open to visitors every Saturday. The gateway in the building adjacent to the wall, led into Henry McDowell's farmyard, while the dark-coloured house was the abode of Captain Pollock, father of Hugh Pollock, Minister of Finance for Northern Ireland in the 1920s.

UPPER MAIN STREET (ii)

This longer view puts the photograph opposite into context. The narrowness of Abbey Street compared with today is evident, as is the interesting mixture of shops and private residences. The house on the extreme right was the manse of First Bangor Presbyterian Church until about 1912

(demolished as a shop in 1972), while on the extreme left can be glimpsed J. S. Balmer Ltd, chemists: "We guarantee all our drugs to be of the finest possible quality, unimpeachable purity and in the finest condition".

HOUSES ON SITE OF TRINITY CHURCH, MAIN STREET

This very old photograph is captioned on the back 'Bowman's House, Main Street'. Trinity Presbyterian Church occupies the site of these houses, which were approached by steps and were remembered for well-kept front gardens. It was reported in 1888 that the landlord the Hon. R. E. Ward was giving compensation of one year's rent to the tenants of the holdings being demolished to accommodate the new church. Charlie Seyers in *Reminiscences of Old Bangor* recalls the houses in the 1860s as being the homes of Ledgerwood and McMillin.

TRINITY PRESBYTERIAN CHURCH, MAIN STREET

Completed in 1889, this new church, in Yorkshire stone, housed the growing Second Bangor congregation who moved from a meeting house in Ash Loanen (Brunswick Road). Its early days were marked by vigorous controversies over now-obscure points of church government, which filled the correspondence pages of the *North Down Herald*. 'High Class Grocer' Abraham Millsopp (right) traded here for a few years then by 1913 had moved up to no. 47. Specialising in tea, he carried on until his death in 1973! Chemist W. P. Doohan (left) was the father of eminent Hollywood actor James Doohan — 'Scotty' of 'Star Trek'!

HAMILTON ROAD PRESBYTERIAN CHURCH

With over 3,000 Presbyterians in Bangor by 1901, the provision of more places of worship was imperative. The church, however, was completed rather hastily amid controversy in 1899. According to W. C. Seyers in *Reminiscences of Old Bangor*, local contractor James Colville failed to finish the job and McLaughlin and Harvey were brought in, but it had also been hinted that not all the money pledged locally was eventually forthcoming. The planned vestibule and tower were not added until 1966 and the unusual glazed roof lantern suggests another compromise.

ROMAN CATHOLIC CHURCH, BRUNSWICK ROAD

Roman Catholics were not numerous in Bangor in this era. The 1901 Census records 424 of that faith out of a population of 5,903. This fine Gothic Revival-style church, dedicated, like the parish church, to St Comgall, was built between 1886 and 1890. The smaller building is probably the earlier chapel of 1851. Before that, an empty house in Ballymagee Street was used for celebrating Mass.

FIRST BANGOR PRESBYTERIAN CHURCH, MAIN STREET

In a unique photograph, the church is seen prior to the addition of the spire in 1881. Presbyterianism has remained staunch in Bangor since the founding of the first congregation by Scotsman Robert Blair in 1623. This handsome building in the 'D'-shaped 'barn' tradition dates from 1831 and superseded a meeting house on the corner of Ballymagee Street and Quay Street. The gentleman in the waistcoat is thought to be James T. Brice (1850–1932) who became the first auctioneer in Bangor in 1881.

PARISH CHURCH AS COMPLETED

By now First Bangor has gained its spire, contractor Sandy McFerran, but the new parish church of 1882 has none! The parish church of St Comgall originated from the growth in Bangor's population and the inconveniently small size of the abbey. The Hon. R. E. Ward of Bangor Castle was the principal benefactor. When the spire was completed in 1899, Dean Edward Maguire, who was rector from 1876 to 1903, ascended quite unconcerned and blessed the topmost stone.

BANGOR HOSPITAL, CASTLE STREET

As completed, the new hospital had uninterrupted views of the countryside! It replaced the outmoded cottage hospital of 1869 (now 82–86 Hamilton Road) and was financed by money raised by public subscription. The foundation stone was laid in 1909 by Miss Emily Connor ('Bangor's Lady Bountiful') who later had the new Connor Wing named after her. Another local philanthropist, Mr W. K. Crosby, declared the building open on 1 October 1910 and the following month public-spirited Councillor John Henderson undertook to supply trees for the grounds.

HOUSE AT JUNCTION OF GRAY'S HILL AND BRYANSBURN ROAD

At first glance this is a very confusing photograph until one realises that the house on the right is long since demolished. It is on the site of the present small roundabout at this busy junction and seems to have disappeared in the early 1920s.

However, very little else has changed. Even the shop on the corner of Dufferin Avenue, and Central Avenue is still called 'West End Stores' eighty years on!

DALMENY HOUSE, 2 DOWNSHIRE ROAD

This is a rare example of an individual photograph of a new Edwardian villa. With its Scottish baronial element, the architecture is not quite typical of Bangor. The architect was Ernest L. Woods, who completed this house about 1905 for Mr John Brown. Woods, also Town Surveyor of Bangor in this era, numbered among other projects the Carnegie Library and the original golf club. He later practised as an architect in Belfast. The house still stands, though with the battlements and ornate gates and gateposts now gone.

THOMAS WILSON AND FAMILY, 'THE BEECHES', 3 DOWNSHIRE ROAD, 1905

The leafy avenues of solid suburban villas, built for the upper middle classes, give inner Bangor a distinctive late Victorian–Edwardian feel: "many new villas attest to its growing favour as a place of residence with businessmen of Belfast" (*Nelson's Thorough Guide to Ireland,* 1909). In this charming 1905 photograph, Belfast shipbroker Thomas Wilson poses with his wife Euphemia, four daughters and guests. A flamboyant man involved in many causes, Thomas Wilson (1863–1930) was knighted in 1922 and became first Mayor of Bangor in 1927.

'MOUNT HERALD' DECORATED FOR 1911 CORONATION

Built around the 1860s for James Skillen, 'Mount Herald' was demolished in 1982 to 'improve' the corner of Clifton Road. Two of Bangor's best-known characters resided here, W. G. Lyttle, editor of the *North Down Herald*, novelist, wit and entertainer (1844–1896), and then James H. Savage (1867–1937) building contractor, councillor, magistrate, philanthropist and sportsman. The Savage firm's biggest job was the Dufferin Memorial Hall, Hamilton Road, in 1905. 'Mount Herald' won first prize for Coronation displays — aptly, as Savage was chairman of the celebration committee!

ULSTER VOLUNTEER FORCE IN 'MOUNT HERALD' YARD, APRIL 1914

This book has concentrated on everyday life in Bangor, but in the years leading up to 1914 there was increasing tension in the background over the possibility of Home Rule for Ireland. German guns were landed at the North Pier from the *s.s. Clydevalley* in April 1914 and this photograph of 'C' Company, U.V.F., was taken just after that event. James H. Savage epitomized the loyalist mind — prepared to confront Crown forces over Ulster's position, but eager once war started to support Britain. Savage was praised for his efforts for soldiers' welfare, which strengthened after the death of his elder son in action in 1917.

THE FIRST MARQUIS OF DUFFERIN AND AVA

Lord Dufferin (1826–1902) has probably been North Down's most eminent figure. His seat was at Ballyleidy, two miles west of Bangor, which he re-modelled and re-named Clandeboye. In memory of his beloved mother, he built Helen's Tower in the demesne in the 1850s, in which are inscribed poems by Browning, Tennyson and others. These and other lofty personages were the society among whom moved Lord Dufferin, diplomat; explorer; author; personal friend and one-time aide to Queen Victoria; Governor-General of Canada; Viceroy of India. Despite his long absences, he took his role as an Irish landlord very seriously and had a deep affection for home.

THE HON. ROBERT EDWARD WARD

The Ward family of Castleward, Co Down, trace their influence
over Bangor affairs to a marriage in 1708 to Anne Hamilton,
the heiress of the Bangor lands. R. E. Ward had the present
Bangor Castle built in 1852. He exerted great influence over
the town's affairs until his death in 1904, owning almost all
the land east of Main Street, and involving himself with many
developments in church, education, and harbour provision. In
class terms, his status as a gentleman of localized importance
contrasts with the distinguished aristocrat Lord Dufferin.
Correspondence between the two reveals that over contentious
land matters Dufferin was quite prepared to be chilly to his
social inferior and address him as 'Dear Ward'.

JOHN McMEEKAN, COUNCIL CHAIRMAN

John McMeekan (1851–1919) seen here as Chairman of the Urban District Council, with the Bangor Fire Brigade, was, according to his obituary, 'for nearly half a century the outstanding figure in Bangor'. Elected chairman for the ruling body an incredible twenty-two times, he presided over, and was often instrumental in, most of the improvements that raised Bangor from an impoverished township struggling to cope with its growth, to a leading resort. McMeekan, who served on Down County Council and in an array of church and official bodies, resided at 19 Farnham Park.

JAMES THOMSON

Also involved in just about every public issue for fifty years
was the redoubtable James Thomson (1855–1945). He and his
outrageous brother Archibald (d.1924) tended either
passionately to support or — more often — implacably oppose
any given scheme. Public meetings frequently ended in
uproar; Archibald summonsed Town Commissioner Robert
Bowman for alleged assault (case dismissed); James bought
Archibald's house for only £50 just before the latter was
bankrupted by libelling McMeekan (more legal repercussions).
The local press constantly reported "Thomsonian
Idiosyncracies"; "Thomsonian Quibbles — Sharp Exchanges",
and, choosing its words carefully, the *Co. Down Spectator* in
its obituary of Archibald, remarked ". . . outside the realm of
church and civic procedure Mr Thomson was a genial and
kindly man". James Thomson, who lived at 'Martello',
Princetown Road, was still involved in the 1930s securing a
good water supply from Ballysallagh.

SAMMY REAVEY

Known affectionately to everyone in Bangor in the last decades of the century was Sammy Reavey of Church Street. For pennies, he would go to the well for people's water and would carry errands in his hat. Walking backwards was another of Sammy's habits. On one occasion, Sammy got lost in Clandeboye Estate and many locals turned out to search for him. His pet phrase was "Would there be a drop o'tay for me?"

JACK SCOTT

Popular Jack Scott was something of a vagrant, who gathered a few pennies by virtue of a fine singing voice. On one occasion he was summonsed by a well-to-do resident for annoying him and jailed briefly, a fate which earned the gentleman adverse comment in the local press. On his death, the Rev. Finlay Maguire and a few friends erected a headstone in the New Cemetery, Newtownards Road.

SAMUEL T. COULTER, CHIEF FIRE OFFICER

Coulter appears to have been an irrepressible personality involved in everything. Joining council service in 1902 he rose to become Sanitary Inspector, being in 1910 the first in Ireland to gain membership of the Royal Sanitary Institute. Here he is seen in another role as Chief Officer of the fire service! A

leading Orangeman, and officer in the Ulster Volunteer Force, he lived at 64 Southwell Road and later May Avenue. Proudly, he was to lead later and grander fire brigades. This hand-cart and its sweating crew were unfortunately the butt of mockery by summer visitors!

HENRY PALFREY, PIERMASTER, 1905

Palfrey (right) held a post in the early years of the century separate to that of Captain Tregaskis, the harbourmaster. One assumes his responsibility was the New Pier, its band concerts and the constant influx of passengers daily in summer. He staged ambitious pageants and pyrotechnic displays and one,

in August 1905, was 'The Relief of Ladysmith', seen here. Palfrey, who lived at 42 Victoria Road, the same summer rescued a Mr Andrews, his wife, child and sister-in-law, whose pleasure boat sank. In the tall hat is William Major, of May Avenue.

DEAN EDWARD MAGUIRE, FIRST RECTOR OF ST COMGALL'S

Dean Edward Maguire played a vital role in the building of St Comgall's. Coming to Bangor in 1876, he realised the abbey was inadequate and urged the select vestry to build a new church rather than repair the old one. Aptly, considering he had also helped choose the site, he was hoisted in a builder's cage to lay his hands on the top of the newly-added spire in 1899. Dean Edward Maguire retired to live in 'Glenbank', Princetown Road, in 1903, the year his son Frederick George (1868–1933) married Clara May Davidson of nearby 'Seacourt', a daughter of the founder of the Sirocco Works, Belfast.

REV J. I. PEACOCKE

Joseph Irvine Peacocke was Dean Edward Maguire's successor at St Comgall's. Very sociable and sporting by nature — as witnessed by this unusual action photograph — he encouraged friendly relations among all denominations in the town. He was also a keen golfer. In 1916, he was elevated to become Bishop of Derry and Raphoe, and his son Cuthbert followed in his footsteps in the same post in 1970.

BILLY TOSH

Bangor like other places had its share of eccentric characters, who were more free, or less cared-for — depending on how you looked at it — than today. Billy Tosh wheeled an empty barrow for company, and was known to wheel it all the way to Belfast to get a wick for a lamp he had on it. McIntosh may have been his correct surname.

JAMES PEDEN

This little man is James Peden, who sold vegetables etc., and herrings in season, from the back of his cart and was what was known as a general dealer. The location is the junction of Church Street and Croft Street. According to a note on the back, the council's foreman lamplighter Bob Stewart (d.1932) lived in the end cottage with gable showing, while the little house in Croft Street showing above the cart was just a mud cabin occupied by a Miss Russell. The date is about 1908. Mr Stewart's sons also became lamplighters.

CHILDREN OF THE MARKET HOUSE SCHOOL, 1874

This school, also known as the 'Ward School', was held in the former market house, nowadays the Northern Bank. The principal (right) was John Gray, a lame man who at one time taught eighty children with no assistance. Here though is a Miss Martin, later Mrs Brown. Among the children are well-known Bangor names notably Ritchie (three), McKee, Gibson and Lowden. The boys with tilted heads in the back row are two brothers named Newman. Seyers recalled Gray in *Reminiscences of Old Bangor,* 'He was my first school master. He taught the "Penny School" where the old market was held . . . He often had a class of young men to learn navigation. He . . . had a short leg and went on a crutch.'

PICNIC AT CLANDEBOYE, c.1910

A note on the back of this photograph explains "Some of First Bangor Presbyterian Church scholars on a picnic at Clandeboye House". The year must be about 1910 and the girls' fashions bear close comparison with the photograph on page 25. The shadows are strong and one can imagine the heat of a summer day, the secluded greenery of the Marquis's demesne, the excitement of the young people — and the total unsuitability of collars, ties and caps!

FOUNDATION OF NEW GAS HOLDER, 1902

Town gas was a boon of Victorian technological progress in which Bangor began to share with the formation of the Bangor Gas Light Co. in 1854. Its first meeting was held in the Royal Hotel. Output was necessarily greater as the town increased in size and here we see expansion underway as a site for a new cylindrical gas holder is begun. Note the steam traction engine and large sieve or riddle for stones. The cottages are situated roughly where Bingham Street now meets Springfield Road.

STAFF OF GAS UNDERTAKING, 1901

Manager Barker Mitchell is seated centre. He served in this capacity for a lifetime, and lived for some fifty years in one of the first houses built in Shandon Drive. The men are (back row left to right): D. Ferris, Wilson Weir, Hugh McMahon, Robert Hanna and Nathaniel Glass. Front row: W. Beattie, John McMahon, Sam Bryant, Sam Kyle and Henry Cousins. By 1915 Kyle had been elevated to meter inspector. Apart from a spell in New Zealand, he and his son spent their working lives in the Gas Department of the council, and his grandson Timothy Kyle was the last gas manager until closure in 1986.

THOMAS HANNA, MASTER PAINTER AND DECORATOR

Thomas Hanna (1855–1932) was based at 116 Ballymagee Street (now High Street) in a house in Irene Terrace. He had a ladder and paint store at the rear in which he allowed local children to play. One of Hanna's hobbies was reproducing scenes of old Bangor in a charming naive style and three such paintings are now in North Down Heritage Centre's collections.

BRICKYARD WORKERS

According to Seyers in *Reminiscences of Old Bangor* the brickfield, part of present-day Ward Park, was approached by a lane from Castle Street, and the bricks that built the pleasant station houses at Cultra and Craigavad came from here.

Standing (left to right): Hugh Harvey, Alex. James, Willie Ward, Tom Rowley, F. Glass, Robert Gibson, W. Gibson, Andy Orr. Sitting: John Gibson, Albert Harvey, W. Anderson, Herbert Orr, A. Gibson, John Orr, Johnnie McCullough.

LOUGHREY'S SHOP, 3 BRIDGE STREET, *c.*1900

'Rosie's Lumps' were delicious confections made by Mrs Loughrey, and were famous during these years of Bangor's heyday. 'Rosie's Stall' on the corner of Main Street and Queen's Parade also sold the sweets. Apparently the younger woman in the foreground is a daughter-in-law of James and

Rosie, who can be seen flanking her. The site was demolished and rebuilt in 1913–14 leaving the holidaymakers only memories. Sir James Craig, first Prime Minister of Northern Ireland, later recalled boyhood enjoyment of 'Rosie's Lumps'.

JAMES LOUGHREY AND HIS CART

Here James Loughrey is seen with his young son at the junction of Somerset Avenue and the seafront walk. The background of the steps and seafront terraces has scarcely altered in over eighty years, since this was taken. By 1915, there were no householders of the name Loughrey in Bangor.

BUILDING THE NEW PIER (i)

Subject of much discussion, this was completed in 1895. Was it primarily to help the commerce of Bangor merchants or provide better facilities for Belfast and other passengers? The latter argument won and a passenger steamer pier was built with a lower deck for low-tide movements. The pitch pine wood was brought specially from Pensacola in Florida and here we can see how the wooden portion was built first, then the concrete section built out to it. When demolished in 1981, many of the timbers were seen to be piled only six or eight feet into the seabed!

BUILDING THE NEW PIER (ii)

Close study of this rare view reveals that contractors H. & J. Martin have built a tramway between the start of the pier and the harbour master's office. Between this and the road they seem to be heaping stones and keeping plant. Bangor in the early 1890s was a ferment of construction and change: the new gardens at Quay Street; the Grand Hotel; Ballyholme promenade; new villas everywhere. The early 1990s parallel that exciting era! The cottage (left) was bought as a wedding present by solicitor George McCracken for his wife, authoress L. A. M. Priestly.

BAKERY CART IN DUFFERIN AVENUE

The delivery man is thought to be David Lytle, who operated a
bakery at 4 Queen's Parade for many years. His ample girth
may testify to the quality of the produce. The house on the
right can be identified even today as No. 64 Dufferin Avenue,
last in a short series of houses with similar stone
ornamentation round the doors. No. 66 has not yet been built.

ON A BUILDING SITE, *c.*1900

The handsome terraces and villas of Bangor appear in hundreds of photographs and postcards, but only very rarely are the men who built them portrayed. Left to right (standing): James McKee, Joseph McCullough, Ralph Briggs, C. Stevenson, David Magowan. (Sitting): A. Gray, Billy Boal. One of James McKee's three sons had fourteen children, so quite a number of Bangor people today are descended from him.

PLOUGHING WITH AN OX

Rural life was very close at hand. The team here is being controlled by Harry Lockhart, on the farm of John Williamson, whose farmhouse is in the background. It stood opposite the Dell at the top of the present Fairfield Road, so this view has probably been taken from a spot near the junction of that road and present-day Broadway. Fairfield Road is a modern name for the first part of Williamson's Lane, a country lane which curved back round to Gransha Road, but is now bisected by the ring road and otherwise encroached upon.

BALLYHOLME WINDMILL, 1887

The windmill on its hilltop site dominated the green fields of Ballyholme and Ballymagee from its construction about 1780 until it was gutted by fire in July 1922. During Victorian times it fell into disuse but was renovated by a miller named McGilton, who may be the gentleman depicted here. The main body of the windmill still stands as a private dwelling, surrounded by more recent housing. So it has withstood the winds, and the winds of change, for much longer even than the span of this book.

ACKNOWLEDGEMENTS

The majority of these photographs have come from North Down Heritage Centre's collections. The important collection of the late Mr Karl Smyth is housed by the Heritage Centre and those reproduced as follows are by courtesy of his brother Mr Bert Smyth: pages 10, 14, 15, 16, 17, 20, 21, 22, 25, 31, 33, 39, 41, 50, 51, 52, 53, 54, 64, 65, 68, 69, 70, 71, 73, 74, 75, 76, 77, 78, 79, 82, 83, 84, 85, 86, 87, 88, 90, 91 and front cover.

Other photographs from the Heritage Centre archives are: pages 7, 8, 13, 27, 29, 36, 37, 40, 48, 56, 57, 58, 59, 61, 67, 72, 80, 81. 'Real Photo' series postcards produced by Hurst and Co., Belfast, are reproduced on pages 18, 55, 57, 60, and back cover. These are now in the Heritage Centre's postcard collection.

The Lawrence Collection photographs on pages 3, 4, 5, 6, 9, 23, 24, 26, 28, 34, 38, 43 and 45 are reproduced by kind permission of the National Library of Ireland, Dublin. The Ulster Museum, Belfast, has given kind permission to reproduce the Welch Collection photographs on pages, 2, 30, 32, 44, 46, 47 and 49, and the Hogg Collection on pages 12 and 19.

The photographs on pages 11, 35, 42, 62 and 66 are courtesy of Dr B. M. Walker and the photograph on page 89 courtesy of Mr M. McKee. The photograph on page 63 is courtesy of Mr T. Jamison.

The author's sincere thanks goes to the following for their kind assistance: Peter Johnson, Tim Kyle, Marshall McKee Sen., John Moore, Bill O'Hara, Marcus Patton, Bert Smyth and Teenie Welham. Gary McCormick of the Heritage Centre has skilfully printed some very old and fragile negatives, while another of my colleagues Sandra Bossence has word-processed the text with care and patience. Thanks also to Jane Crosbie and Margaret McNulty of Friar's Bush Press for their constant interest and encouragement.

SOURCES

No one book exists on the whole period of Bangor's history. However, the following publications have all provided useful material: *Historic Buildings in Bangor and Groomsport* by Marcus Patton (Ulster Architectural Heritage Society, Belfast, 1984); *Victorian Bangor* ed. Grenfell Morton (Queen's University, Belfast, 1972); *The Bangor Season* ed. W. G. Lyttle (Bangor, 1885, reprint Belfast *ca.* 1980); *A Tour of North Down* by Jane E. M. Crosbie (Belfast, 1989); *My Bangor* by C. F. Milligan (Bangor, 1975); *Reminiscences of Old Bangor* by W. C. Seyers (original articles in *Co. Down Spectator* of 1932 and 1933 reprinted in book form, Belfast 1983). The three journals produced by Bangor Historical Society between 1981 and 1984 have also been consulted.

Back numbers of the *Co. Down Spectator*, which began publication in 1904, have been widely consulted. Only cuttings books for W. G. Lyttle's *North Down Herald* exist locally in the Heritage Centre archives, but they have yielded much of interest. The street directories produced by the *Spectator* and the splendid *Official Guide*, undated but about 1910, have been much used.